The Christian Walk:
Seven Steps to Living for Jesus

Steve Kelly

Copyright © Wave Church, Inc. & Wave Publishing LLC, 2013.

All rights reserved. No portion of this book may be reproduced, stored in a retrieval system, or transmitted in any form or by any means, without the prior written permission of the publisher.

Table of Contents

Introduction	5
Step 1 – Salvation	11
Step 2 – Water Baptism	21
Step 3 – Holy Spirit	25
Step 4 – Bible Study	33
Step 5 – Daily Prayer	39
Step 6 – Church	45
Step 7 – Generosity	51

Introduction

A single right decision can change a life. A single right decision can transform a family. Some decisions, like the one made over thirty years ago on a scorching summer day in Penrith, Australia, can literally influence generations.

His palms were sweating. His heart was pounding. A half-drunk teenager, he looked to his left and right. His two old drinking mates looked straight ahead, their mouths moving in silent prayer. He was in a church, of all places. He'd not chosen to be here. He *never* would have chosen to be here.

Now he felt himself *choosing* to answer the preacher's call to trust in God. He had ever only trusted himself, yet he stood and began to walk the aisle to give His life to Jesus. He stared at his feet as they slowly led him forward. How was this happening?

A few hours earlier, those two buddies – who'd gotten into scraps with him, who'd plowed through shots of liquor and fallen down laughing with him – had shown up at his parent's house and forced him into their beat-up car. They told him he owed it to them to go with them. *Just this once*, they said.

So he got in the car, despite feeling a good buzz (or maybe

because of it) from the beers he'd pounded while tinkering on his own beat-up car. He got in their car despite sporting a black eye from a recent fight, despite the grease and oil all over his arms and his tank top and shorts. Surely they wouldn't *really* take him to church *looking* like this. *Feeling* like this.

As they drove, he could hear them praying. Praying for him. The nerve! As if he needed their prayers. He was doing fine. Church and God were for weaklings. He flexed his right arm; the same right arm that had knocked out the guy who gave him that black eye. Knocked him out cold. Yeah, God was for weaklings, and he was definitely not a weakling.

Now he found himself in the front of the church crowd, after a three-hour service full of singing and preaching. What a bunch of nonsense, he had thought. Yet, there he stood, right under the nose of the preacher, a man named A.S. Worley.

He looked around. Others had walked forward, just like him. Some were crying, some were smiling, but all of them felt something different. Something unexplainable. God's unconditional love.

"God has a plan for you," he heard Pastor Worley say. "I'm talking to you, young man, yes you, in the tank top. With the black eye." The preacher was talking to him. In front of *everyone*. He looked down but the preacher continued.

As Pastor Worley spoke, the young man lifted his face. With each word, he felt a growing sense of agreement with the preacher.

Pastor Worley told him that he would be a key Christian youth leader in the city of Sydney. That day, the hard-headed and heavy-hearted teenage alcoholic surrendered his life to Jesus. As the days passed, he remembered the words of Pastor Worley, and he became a preacher of the gospel. A pastor.

That was January 1981, and that boy was me, Steve Kelly. You see; the decision to follow Jesus can change everything. I was a troublemaker headed for a life of trouble when Jesus found me. He found me because two good friends stopped me from walking down the path I was on. Since that day, I've been on the Christian Walk, living for Jesus.

No matter where you come from, or what you've done, Jesus loves you. He gave His life for you, and He will guide you down the path of truth and joy as you live for Him.

It's not always easy, but one key thing to remember is that He's forgiven you of your past. I should know – my past is riddled with problems.

I was born in New York City, the third of five children born to alcoholic parents. I was eight years old when my parents took our family out of the country because of all their problems. I remember desperately wishing we could stay in America. I even promised myself that one day I would return.

We moved to Sydney, Australia, without any friends or family. My parents continued drinking, and soon my older brothers picked up the habit. The next ten years was awful, but the day I accepted Jesus, everything changed. Over the next several years, my parents became Christians and got sober. My brothers and sisters also gave their lives to Jesus.

I became a pastor at the church where I made the decision to follow Jesus. After ten years, I became the Executive Director for what is now Hillsong College, and then I became the Senior Associate Pastor for Hills Christian Life Centre. After eight years, with the blessing of Brian and Bobbie Houston, I came to America to pastor Wave Church. Little did I know as a terrified eight-year-old leaving New York, God had it planned for me to return to the United States and preach His Word. All I had to do was decide to follow Him.

It's the best decision I've ever made. **It's the best decision you'll ever make.** Whether you're just beginning life with Jesus, or you've stumbled and are getting back on the road with Jesus, welcome to where you belong. It is my sincere hope and prayer that this booklet gives you answers and strength for each moment of your Christian Walk.

God is ready to guide you on the journey of your life. Like a father to His child (and you are His), He wants to take your hand and lead you down the path ahead.

He wants to guide you on this journey.

He wants to show you where to walk.

He wants to cheer you on as you run.

Let's get started on Your Walk.

The Christian Walk:
Seven Steps to Living for Jesus.

Sincerely,
Steve Kelly
Senior Pastor, Wave Church

Step One: Salvation

As mentioned in the introduction, Jesus gave His life so that you – and every other person on Earth – would never have to walk through life alone. Before His sacrifice, humanity was separated from God. After His crucifixion, we were able to re-unite with our Creator. Accepting Jesus gives us access to the life God intended millennia ago when he first breathed life into Adam and Eve.

Because of God's amazing grace, we are able to enter into relationship with Him. Ephesians 2:8-9 explains this remarkable gift, which is impossible to earn and without which it is impossible to be saved:

"For by grace you have been saved through faith, and that not of yourselves: *it is the gift of God, not of works*, lest anyone should boast."

God's love is so relentless, so unstoppable, so perfect, that He accepts us as we are. He not only sent Jesus to die to redeem us and restore our relationship with Himself, but He also provides the grace needed for us to comprehend and accept His salvation.

The Message Translation of the Bible explains this incredible truth so well that the entire passage of Ephesians 2:1-10, written by the Apostle Paul, is included here. **Please**

read this passage a few times. It is a powerful expression of how desperate our need for Jesus is and how God's grace gives us eternal life.

It wasn't so long ago that you were mired in that old stagnant life of sin. You let the world, which doesn't know the first thing about living, tell you how to live. You filled your lungs with polluted unbelief, and then exhaled disobedience.

We all did it, all of us doing what we felt like doing, when we felt like doing it, all of us in the same boat. It's a wonder God didn't lose his temper and do away with the whole lot of us. Instead, immense in mercy and with an incredible love, He embraced us. He took our sin-dead lives and made us alive in Christ. He did all this on his own, with no help from us! Then He picked us up and set us down in highest heaven in company with Jesus, our Messiah…

Saving is all His idea, *and all His work. All we do is trust Him enough to let him do it. It's God's gift from start to finish! We don't play the major role. If we did, we'd probably go around bragging that we'd done the whole thing! No, we neither make nor save ourselves. God does both the making and saving. He creates each of us by Christ Jesus to join Him in the work he does, the good work He has gotten ready for us to do, work we had better be doing.*

You prayed to invite Jesus into your life. You believe in your heart that God raised Jesus from the dead. His grace makes you a Christian. The Bible promises that this step of confession and belief rescues you from the emptiness of a lonely life. As a result, you receive eternal salvation and present purpose for the rest of your days.[1]

But there is much more to the Christian life than praying to accept Jesus Christ. Living for Jesus is not a one-time encounter. It is a lifestyle. It is a daily walk of obedience and worship, of faithfulness and surrender to His will.

The following pages will help you understand your relationship with God and your purpose in life. They will help you follow Jesus, and ultimately, become like Him.

Before moving on, however; it's helpful to understand how it came to be that you could receive eternal salvation through praying and believing that Jesus was God's Son and that He lived a sinless life, that He died on the cross for our sins and He rose from the dead to secure eternal life for all who believe.[2]

How is it that Jesus came to Earth? How is it that He was born of a virgin, was raised by Mary and her carpenter husband Joseph[3], performed amazing miracles[4], and sacrificed Himself for the sins of the world?

---

1 *Romans 10:9-10*
2 *John 3:16*
3 *Luke 1:26 – 2:20*
4 *John 11:38-45*

It all began a long time ago in a place called Eden. In Eden, the world was perfect. Adam and Eve were in perfect relationship with God. They were given control over all the animals and plants. They were allowed to eat anything, except for the fruit of the tree of the knowledge of good and evil. If they ate of it, God told them they would die.[5]

For a while, they obeyed. They left the tree alone because that was God's command. Eventually, they ignored God's directions and they ate the fruit of the tree.

As soon as they violated the one rule that God gave them, they violated the perfect trust He had in them. And they knew things were forever changed. They hid from God because they were ashamed[6] of their disobedience. This same instinct lives on today.

We've all seen children hide when they disobey. Grown-ups do it too; we're just better at covering our tracks.

They hid because they disobeyed. More than anything, God desires obedience. It is the best evidence of our trust and faith in Him. He knows what is best for our lives and He will always guide us to do what will ultimately be best for our lives. He desires obedience even more than personal sacrifice or worship.[7]

---

5   *Genesis 2:17*
6   *Genesis 3:8*
7   *I Samuel 15:22*

Obedience is the ultimate demonstration of our devotion to God. God had no recourse but to banish Adam and Eve from the Garden. His rule said, "If you eat of the Tree, you will die."[8] His perfection could not accommodate a second chance.

The dying process began that day, not just for Adam and Eve but also for every creature.

Over time, the generations grew further away from God as the compounding effects of sin led to more covering up and ultimately more hiding from the one God who loved them more than anyone else.

Sin entered the world through Adam and Eve's disobedience.[9] It served as a barrier between God and Man for thousands of years.

The great news is, because of Jesus, we are no longer separated by sin from a relationship with God. The Bible tells us in Galatians 4:4-5, "But when the fullness of time had come, God sent forth His Son, born of a woman… to redeem those born under the law, that we might receive the adoption of sons."

Jesus, in complete obedience to God the Father, left Heaven and came to Earth to atone for the disobedience

---

8 *Genesis 2:17*
9 *Romans 5:12*

that severed man's ability to have a direct relationship with God.[10]

This man, Jesus (who was also God), walked a path no one else could walk to give the rest of humanity the only path to a re-connected relationship with God.

You see, long before you made your choice to accept Jesus, Jesus made the choice to accept God's plan to rescue mankind from his sins. He gave Himself to redeem us.[11]

Almost everybody has heard of John 3:16, which reads, "For God so loved the world, He gave His only Son (Jesus), that whoever believes in Him should not perish, but have everlasting life."

As this verse testifies, it was God's love that sent Jesus to the cross.

God's remarkable, transforming, overwhelming love for every person on Earth caused Him to send His only Son to make up for the disobedience of Adam and Eve.

The apostle Paul (who wrote 60% of the New Testament) wrote the following words to describe God's love:

| 10 | I John 4:10 |
| 11 | Titus 2:14 |

*I am sure that neither death nor life, nor angels nor rulers,
nor things present nor things to come, nor powers,
nor height nor depth, nor anything else in creation, will be
able to separate us from the love of God in Christ Jesus our
Lord.*[12]

Another great passage, I John 3:1 says, "How great is the love the Father has lavished upon us, that we should be called the children of God! And that is what we are!"

By accepting Jesus, you have been adopted as God's son or daughter. In fact, all who believe are called "joint heirs with Christ."[13]

To be a joint heir means to inherit everything that Jesus has through God. Your decision to trust Jesus gives you access to the "unfathomable riches of Christ."[14]

Think about that. Through Jesus's sacrifice, you are now joined to the God of all Creation. You not only get to walk with God, you get all you need to walk for God.

The following verses describe just a few benefits that are found in being adopted into the family of God. These scriptures explain just some of the blessings of being a "joint heir with Jesus Christ."

---

12   *Romans 8:37-39*
13   *Romans 8:17*
14   *Ephesians 3:8*

John 1:12 – "As many as receive Him, to them He gave power to become the sons of God."

John 3:36 – "He that believes on the Son has everlasting life; and he that does not believe on the Son will not see life, but the wrath of God…"

John 8:12 – "Then Jesus spoke unto them saying, I am the light of the world: he that follows me will not walk in darkness but will have the light of life."

Accepting Jesus as your Savior gives you light for the path ahead. **His sacrifice brought you out of the shadows of shame.** He redeemed your life by giving His own. He made a way where there was no way. He is the only way to eternal salvation. Your declaration of Him as Lord, your belief in Him and confession of your sins has made you a new person.

You've found your home in Jesus. You've been adopted into the family of God. You're born again. He has cleansed you from all your sins, just as He promised.[15]

You aren't the same person you were when you found - rather - when Jesus found you.[16]

---

15   *I John 1:9*
16   *John 15:16*

You are not the same person who asked for His forgiveness of sin. You are a new creation![17] Before you invited Him to take control of your life, you were ruled by your ambition, your lust. What John describes as the "desires of the flesh."[18]

A seemingly unlimited number of base desires and fleshly forces drove you to choose things that ultimately left you even more empty and tired than you were the day before.

Now, you find power in Him, light for the path ahead, and strength to walk the walk of faith. The Walk of following Jesus is underway. You've taken the first step – accepting Jesus as your Savior. The rest of this book helps you take the next steps in this journey to become like Jesus.

---

17   *2 Corinthians 5:17*
18   *1 John 2:16*

Step Two: Water Baptism

In the preceding pages, God's desire for obedience was mentioned more than once. This is because God truly desires obedience above all else. The disobedience of the nation of Israel, as written about through the Old Testament, was the primary cause of their problems.

Likewise, when Christians disobey God, they experience problems. God doesn't cause these problems; they are caused by our decision to violate God's rules. It's vital to understand, whether you've been a Christian for one day or fifty years, that obedience to God is the surest and best way to walk in His goodness and to receive His best for your life.[19]

One very important way that we show our obedience to God is through the act of being baptized in water. Jesus was baptized by John the Baptist (yes, that's how he got his name) to show obedience to God.

As the Bible explains in Matthew 3:13-17, "Then Jesus came from Galilee to John at the Jordan to be baptized by him. And John tried to prevent Him, saying, 'I need to be baptized by You, and are You coming to me?'

---

[19] *Deuteronomy 28:1-14*

But Jesus answered and said to him, 'Permit it to be so now, for thus it is fitting for us to fulfill all righteousness.' Then John allowed Him. When He had been baptized, Jesus came up immediately from the water; and behold, the heavens were opened to Him, and He saw the Spirit of God descending like a dove and alighting upon Him. And suddenly a voice came from heaven, saying, 'This is My beloved Son, in whom I am well pleased.'"

God was "well pleased" with Jesus's obedient act of being baptized. For the Christian, this symbolic gesture not only serves to demonstrate our obedience to God, it also tells the world that we have chosen to identify with Jesus in three key ways:

1. By being lowered in the water, we identify with the death of Christ.
2. By being submerged in the water, we identify with the burial of Christ.
3. By being lifted out of the water, we identify with the resurrection of Christ, and the new life in Him.

Water baptism gives an opportunity to declare to others that we are fully surrendered to God. We have been symbolically "crucified with Christ, and no longer is it me that lives, but Christ who lives in me; and the life which I now live in the flesh I live by faith in the Son of God, who loved me and gave Himself for me."[20]

---

20 *Galatians 2:20*

Baptism is a sign of obedience. It's a symbol of our commitment to Christ and our identification with His death, burial and resurrection. But what does it mean?

Baptism literally means "washing". It demonstrates a washing away of all sin and the cleansing power of Jesus to forgive and forget what was done in the past and to establish a clean slate for the future. Jesus has already forgiven your sins but this is a ceremony that serves as a reminder to your heart and an announcement to the world. Jesus is your Lord.

Baptism is very important. The apostle Peter told the early believers that they must, "Repent *and* be baptized, every one of you, in the name of Jesus Christ for the forgiveness of your sins."[21]

Water baptism is a vital part of becoming a follower of Christ. It shows you are truly obedient to His plan and it lets the world know that you are clean and changed, and you are forevermore following Him.

---

21   *Acts 2:38*

Step Three:
Baptism of the Holy Spirit

As you now know, Jesus came to Earth, lived and died so that we all might be saved. God loved us so much; He gave His only Son for us.

As Dietrich Bonhoeffer put it, "You were bought with a price, and **what has cost God much cannot be cheap**. For the sake of each of us He laid down His life…no less than the universe."

Because of His tremendous sacrifice, once we were redeemed, God had no intention of leaving us to our own devices. After Jesus rose from the dead, He prepared to leave Earth and return to Heaven to be with God the Father.

Before He left, however, He explained to the disciples and other believers that He would fulfill His earlier promise regarding His coming to Earth: "I have come that you might have life, and that you might have it in abundance."[22]

The early Christians were gathered as Jesus readied them for His departure. Here is what transpired, as recorded by Luke in the book of Acts:

---

[22] *John 10:10*

And being assembled together with them, He (Jesus) commanded them not to depart from Jerusalem, but to wait for the Promise of the Father, "which," He said, "you have heard from Me; for John truly baptized with water, but you shall be baptized with the Holy Spirit not many days from now."... But you shall receive power when the Holy Spirit has come upon you and you will be witnesses to Me in Jerusalem, and in all Judea and Samaria, and to the end of the earth.[23]

Jesus knew that once He left, which He did after He said those words above, the believers would be in need of strength and power. After all, they were going to go to the "end of the earth". That's a long journey, especially back before airplanes and cars were invented!

Not only did Jesus promise that we'd have an abundant life, He also promised that we would be able to do greater things than He did.[24]

That's a bold statement. Jesus turned water into wine;[25] he gave sight to the blind.[26] He even raised the dead![27] And yet, He said we would have the power to do all these things.

And, as the book of Acts tells us, the apostles were

23	Acts 1:4-5, 8
24	John 14:12
25	John 2:1-11
26	Mark 8:22-26
27	Mark 5:35-43

equipped with the power to perform miracles, even the raising of the dead.[28]

How was this possible? ***How is this possible?***

Let's continue reading in Acts. After Jesus left Earth, the disciples were gathered in a building, waiting, as Jesus instructed them, for the Holy Spirit. Jesus had already explained that there was a difference between baptism in water and the baptism of the Holy Spirit.

So, they were waiting. And then, it happened.

They were all together in one place. Suddenly, a sound like the blowing of a violent wind came from heaven and filled the whole house where they were sitting. They saw what seemed to be tongues of fire that separated and came to rest on each of them. ALL of them were FILLED with the Holy Spirit and began to speak in other tongues as the Spirit enabled them.[29]

They received the baptism of the Holy Spirit and spoke in other tongues. They received the power that comes from having the living Spirit of God inside. As they began to walk each day with the permanent presence of the Holy Spirit, they were empowered to take the gospel to the end of the earth.

---

28   *Acts 20:7-12*
29   *Acts 2:1-4*

The baptism of the Holy Spirit is a separate and distinct work of God. It is not the act of salvation through faith; it is not the act of being baptized in water to show obedience. The baptism of the Holy Spirit is a transfer of power, as Jesus promised. The Holy Spirit is the third part of God. God consists of the Father, the Son (Jesus) and the Holy Spirit.

The Holy Spirit gave Jesus the power to overcome Satan.[30] The Holy Spirit is sent to teach us, to remind us of what Jesus did.[31] **The Holy Spirit is the activating force for Christians to walk unashamed, unafraid through life.**

When you are baptized with water, you get wet. The water dripping from your hair and skin is evidence that you were baptized. The baptism of the Holy Spirit also produces physical evidence.

The evidence of the baptism of the Holy Spirit is through the gift, from God, of a prayer language. Your prayer language, or "tongue", is a unique pattern of sounds that may sound like a foreign language. This foreign language sounds different and may even feel unusual at first.

Just like the early believers in the book of Acts, you will speak in this tongue as the Spirit enables you. Over time, it begins to feel quite natural, and in fact, necessary.

---

30 *Luke 4:1*
31 *John 14:26*

The reason it feels different is because you are uttering a language that is not of this earth. It is literally the Holy Spirit, speaking to God, through you.[32] **Your prayer language is the Holy Spirit praying through you, for you.**

The Holy Spirit is God's gift to you. Jesus explained this in Luke 11:11-13:

Which of you fathers, if your son asks for a fish, will give him a snake instead? Or if he asks for an egg, will give him a scorpion? If you then, who are evil, know how to give good gifts to your children, how much more will your Father in Heaven give the Holy Spirit to those who ask him!

As a new believer, you should desire this gift from God. And just like a child to his earthly father, all you have to do is ask Him! When we don't know how to pray, this prayer language enables the Holy Spirit to pray God's will through us. It's a wonderful blessing from God. And it's for every Christian. And it's for you, today.

So, how do you receive it?

Let's turn to God's Word for the answer. After the initial baptism of the Holy Spirit on the Day of Pentecost (the day described in Acts 2, above), other men and women desired the power that came from the baptism of the Holy Spirit.

---

[32] *Romans 8:26-27*

A great illustration of this transfer of the Holy Spirit is outlined in Acts 19:1-6. The apostle Paul was in Ephesus, an ancient city located in the country we now call Turkey. He approached some new Christians and had the following conversation:

> **Paul:** Did you receive the Holy Spirit when you believed?
>
> **New Christians:** We have not heard that there is a Holy Spirit.
>
> **Paul:** Into what then were you baptized?
>
> **New Christians:** John's baptism (water baptism).
>
> **Paul:** John indeed baptized with a baptism of repentance, saying to the people that they should believe on Him who would come after him. That is, believe on Christ Jesus.

When they heard this, they were baptized in the name of the Lord Jesus. And when Paul had laid hands on them, the Holy Spirit came upon them and they spoke with tongues and prophesied.

Maybe, like the people in this story, you have not yet heard that there is a Holy Spirit. Now you know. The Holy Spirit is essential for the Christian to walk at full strength. The Baptism of the Holy Spirit will give you power to endure and thrive in modern life.

If you are attending a Spirit-filled church, simply ask a pastor about the Baptism of the Holy Spirit. He or she will be able to explain in more detail and when you're ready, lay hands on you, just as Paul did two thousand years ago, and pray for you to receive the full compliment of God's power for your life through this amazing gift.

It's been quite a walk already and you're just getting started.

Let's recap everything that's happened so far.

You've taken major steps in your walk of faith in Jesus Christ.

1. You've accepted Jesus as your Savior.
2. You have been water baptized.
3. You've received the baptism of the Holy Spirit.

These are significant, life-transforming events! While each of them is essential for a complete and full Christian walk, they are one-time events. They are big steps, but they are single steps. The rest of this book deals with the daily steps from here on out that not only keeps you on the right path, but also helps you walk the walk, straight and true.

While the first three steps happen in order: salvation, followed by the two baptisms, the rest of the steps in this book happen concurrently. **Together, the remaining steps, taken on a regular basis, ensure that you can truly walk The Walk.**

Step Four: Bible Study

Before GPS, people used paper maps to chart their course or plot their path. In the Christian Walk, the map that we have been given is the greatest book ever written. It's no coincidence that it's the greatest selling book of all time. It's the Bible. God's Word.

The Bible is full of all the information you'd find on a map. It contains checkpoints to ensure you're headed in the right direction. For example, the book of Philippians, the eleventh book in the New Testament, provides an outline of how to "work out your salvation with fear and trembling".[33]

We do this by following the steps outlined in the balance of that chapter: (1) Remember that God is working in you to do His will, (2) Do everything without complaint so that you will be a good example for God and a light to the world, and (3) Hold firmly to the word of life.

These instructions occur in verses 13-16. The preceding paragraphs are a simple illustration of Bible study. Look up the passage in your Bible now and review it. Consider what it says. Think deeply about what it means and how you can apply its advice to your daily walk.

---

[33] *Philippians 2:12*

There's no reason to be intimidated by the Bible. Every word is inspired by God and every word is to be used for your improvement and guidance.

"Every Scripture is given by inspiration of God, and is profitable for doctrine, for reproof, for correction, for instruction in righteousness, that the man of God may be complete, thoroughly equipped for every good work."[34]

In addition to technical direction for your daily walk, the Bible also has examples of pioneers. Trail blazers. **It's filled with stories of people who have walked the walk before you, and from whom you can learn, take heart and be encouraged to keep going.** The book of Daniel, in the Old Testament, contains a story of three young men who were forced to choose between obeying God and obeying a wicked king named Nebuchadnezzar. The following story comes from Daniel 3:1-25.

King Nebuchadnezzar was the king of Babylon and his nation had conquered the people of Israel and he took the brightest young Israelites to serve in the palace and throughout the kingdom.

He decreed that all the people were to bow down to a giant golden statue of him. Three young men, Shadrach, Meshach and Abed-Nego, refused to bow. They told the king they would only bow to the one true God.

---

34   2 Timothy 3:16

King Nebuchadnezzar became furious and told them to bow before him or be thrown into a giant fiery furnace. They still refused, and were taken to the furnace to be burned alive. The fire was so hot it killed the soldiers who tossed Shadrach, Meshach and Abed-Nego into the furnace.

To the king's amazement and shock, as he looked into the furnace, not only were the three young men not burned, they were walking around, and a fourth man had joined them in the fire!

In verse 25, King Nebuchadnezzar declares, "Look! I see four men loose, walking in the midst of the fire; and they are not hurt, and the form of the fourth is like the Son of God."

Jesus walked with the faithful young men in the fire. He protected them and comforted them. Along your walk, you may encounter dangerous circumstances that test your faith. It's inspiring to read of other believers who trusted God. It's inspiring to know that Jesus will walk with you through whatever fire you may face.

These two examples, one from the Old Testament, one from the New, are given to show you the richness and diversity of the Word of God. The Bible is full, from cover to cover, of amazing truths, powerful stories and compelling examples that all serve as a map for your Christian walk.

The more frequently you refer to the Bible, the more likely you are to stay on course.

It's good to know how to use your map. Here are some basics about the Word of God:

The Bible is made of sixty-six books. They are separated into two sections, the Old Testament and the New Testament. The Old Testament has thirty-nine books. The New Testament has twenty-seven books, many of which were written by the Apostle Paul. (Apostle is a word for someone who is a significant church leader. An apostle is a man or woman who has been appointed by God, as evidenced by their gifting, instruction, and leadership to oversee a geographical region)

The chart on the next page is very helpful to understand the types of books as defined by their content.

BOOKS OF THE BIBLE

OLD TESTAMENT – 39 BOOKS

LAW – 5	POETRY – 5	MAJOR PROPHETS – 5
GENESIS	JOB	ISAIAH
EXODUS	PSALMS	JEREMIAH
LEVITICUS	PROVERBS	LAMENTATIONS
NUMBERS	ECCLESIASTES	EZEKIEL
DEUTERONOMY	SONG OF SOLOMON	DANIEL

HISTORY – 12		MINOR PROPHETS – 12
JOSHUA		HOSEA
JUDGES		JOEL
RUTH		AMOS
1 SAMUEL		OBADIAH
2 SAMUEL		JONAH
1 KINGS		MICAH
2 KINGS		NAHUM
1 CHRONICLES		HABUKKUK
2 CHRONICLES		ZEPHANIAH
EZRA		HAGGAI
NEHEMIAH		ZECHARIAH
ESTHER		MALACHI

NEW TESTAMENT – 27 BOOKS

GOSPELS – 4	PAULS LETTERS TO FRIENDS – 4
MATTHEW	1 TIMOTHY
MARK	2 TIMOTHY
LUKE	TITUS
JOHN	PHILEMON

HISTORY – 1
ACTS

PAULS LETTERS TO CHURCHES – 9	GENERAL LETTERS – 9
ROMANS	HEBREWS
1 CORINTHIANS	JAMES
2 CORINTHIANS	1 PETER
GALATIANS	2 PETER
EPHESIANS	1 JOHN
PHILIPPIANS	2 JOHN
COLOSSIANS	3 JOHN
1 THESSALONIANS	JUDE
2 THESSALONIANS	REVELATION

As you can see, the Bible has many books covering a variety of topics and written in different styles. Many people often ask where to begin. There are lots of Bible reading schedules available online. Many pastors recommend the book of John, the fourth book of the New Testament, to help you understand more about Jesus' life and what He expects of you. Others recommend the book of Psalms (Old Testament – in the middle) for encouragement, the book of Proverbs (next to Psalms) for wisdom, and the books of Romans and I Corinthians (sixth and seventh books of the New Testament) to help you understand the general principles for living as a Christian.

All of these suggestions are helpful. **The most important part is that you read the Bible regularly**. Over time, you'll discover it contains answers and encouragement, correction and direction for every area of your life.

The step of Bible study is essential for your growth as a Christian. It is essential for providing you with the map for your walk. Stay committed to Bible reading and you will find your steps ordered by the Lord.[35]

---

35   *Psalm 37:23*

Step Five: Daily Prayer

"Prayer is the way that the life of God in us is nourished. We look upon prayer simply as a means of getting things for ourselves, but **the biblical purpose of prayer is that we may get to know God Himself**."[36]

As this quote illustrates, prayer is often perceived as a way to ask God for things. The reality is prayer is not about changing things around us so much as it is about changing us so that we can then be agents of change to the world around us.

And prayer is easy. Really easy. Prayer is simply talking to God. It's a conversation with your heavenly Father.

Jesus himself directly explains the components of prayer in Matthew 6:9-13. This passage contains what most people call The Lord's Prayer. It has seven distinct elements that provide understanding for the Christian in both how to pray and what to pray. The seven elements are underlined, and the corresponding language from the prayer is in parentheses, as follows:

1. Give reverence to God (Holy is Your name)

2. Surrender to His will (Your Kingdom come)

---

[36] *Chambers, Oswald. My Utmost for His Highest*

3. <u>Ask God to Provide Today's Needs</u> (Give us this day our daily bread)

4. <u>Practice Forgiveness and be Forgiven</u> (forgive us as we forgive those who've offended us)

5. <u>Request Protection from Temptation</u> (lead us not into temptation, but deliver us from evil)

6. <u>Accept God's Authority</u> (for Yours is the Kingdom and the power and the glory forever)

7. <u>Agree with God</u> (Amen)

These steps can be used as a model for prayer. Over time, you will develop your own style of conversation with God, but it is important to remember these steps. Approach God candidly and truthfully, but do not approach Him without deference and due respect. He is open to anything and everything that is on your heart, but He is still God and deserves nothing more than our utmost respect.

As much as The Lord's Prayer is a model, there is no formula for prayer. There is no time limit. In fact, Paul says we should "Pray continually."[37]

---

37   *I Thessalonians 5:17*

His instruction is meant to encourage you to understand that you can pray anywhere, at any time.

The wonder of prayer is that it is an instant, direct link between your heart and God.

There are times when you will pray for a minute or two. There are times when you may pray for an hour or more.

Beyond The Lord's Prayer, the Bible explains prayer in many passages as having many purposes:

Jeremiah 33:3 – Call unto me and I will answer you, and show you great and mighty things.

*Matthew 5:44 – Love your enemies, bless them that curse you, do good to them that hate you, and **pray for them who persecute you.***

*James 5:15-16 – And the prayer of faith shall save the sick, and the Lord will raise him up; and if he has committed sins, they will be forgiven him. Confess your faults one to another, and pray one for another, that you may be healed. **The effectual fervent prayer of a righteous man accomplishes much.***

As these verses illustrate, there are times to pray for yourself, and times to pray for others – including your enemies.

Whatever the purpose, **daily prayer helps align your spirit with God, and helps illuminate your path as you walk the road of the faithful Christian life**.

Praying in the Spirit

The preceding pages explain the purpose of prayer in your earthly language. There is another type of prayer, which was alluded to in the section on the Baptism of the Holy Spirit - praying in your heavenly prayer language, also called Praying in the Spirit.

Praying in the Spirit is designed to edify the Christian.

In I Corinthians 14:4, Paul writes about the power and purpose of this gift. He says, "He who speaks in a tongue edifies himself."

Further, this entire passage contains additional understanding for us in praying in the Spirit. Paul explains how it strengthens your spirit but does not benefit anyone else.

He writes, "unless I speak words easy to understand, how will it be known what is spoken?"[38]

So, it's clear that praying in the Spirit is personal. It's designed to be done to encourage your inner spirit. You might think that means it should be done rarely. That is

---

38   *I Corinthians 14:9*

not the case at all. In fact, because it is personal, praying in the Spirit should be done all the time, and it can be done all the time.

Even though Paul makes it clear that praying in the Spirit is not designed to help others, he also makes it clear that it is essential for power in your Christian walk.

He continues near the end of the chapter, and sums up his opinion on praying in the Spirit in verses 18-19, when he writes, "I thank my God that I speak in tongues more than you all."

Praying in the Spirit is one of the most powerful methods a Christian has to gain strength for each day. And in moments of crisis or confusion, praying in the Spirit enables you to pray the perfect will of God.

"…for we know not how to pray as we ought; but the Spirit himself makes intercession for us with groanings (our prayer language) which cannot be uttered; and He that searches the hearts knows what is the mind of the spirit, because He makes intercession for the saints according to the will of God."[39]

Praying in the Spirit is a habit every Christian should keep.

---

[39] *Romans 8:26*

By daily praying with your natural language, and by daily praying in the Spirit, you will combine every avenue of communication with God, and will thereby strengthen yourself in every possible way.

Gaining this strength will keep you on course, attentive to His voice and moving forward every day along the walk of faith in God. Make every effort to include daily prayer in your Christian walk.

Step Six: The Local Church

When Jesus left Earth, He sent the Holy Spirit, as you have already read. He also instituted a plan for reaching others. He knew we were made to be in relationships. Not only with God but also with other men and women.

God recognized man's need for social connection at the very beginning. In Genesis 2:18, after God created Adam, and saw him alone in the Garden of Eden, God remarked, "It is not good that the man should be alone; I will make a helpmate for him." And God created Eve.

This need for relationship that began with Adam and Eve continued throughout the history of humanity and is alive and well today.

In our relationships we find joy, encouragement, love, inspiration, support and strength. As a Christian, the most important relationships are found by getting connected to a local, Bible-based, life-giving church.

God's plan to provide you with the strength to walk the Walk is founded upon strong relationships in the local church. Jesus declared that the church is the most powerful force on earth, more powerful than the enemies of God.

When Peter correctly said that Jesus was the Son of God, Jesus replied that this revelation is the rock upon which He would build His church, "and the gates of Hades will not prevail against it."[40]

The local church is a community of believers. Jesus commanded that Christians "forsake not gathering together"[41] to worship and learn more about what God desires. God declared that the church is His strategy for Christians to work together, to support one another, to build His plan on earth until He returns.

The church is the hope of the world. God instituted the church to be the one thing that nothing can stop. The church has faced persecution, attack, and defamation for the past 2,000 years, and she has never disappeared. She continues to be the greatest source of help to mankind because the church is the only true source of lasting help.

The Bible promises that those who are regular and active in church will have a life that grows and improves.

Psalm 92:13 says, "Those who are planted in the House of the Lord will flourish." It's interesting that the writer uses the word *planted* to describe a person's connection to the church.

---

40   *Matthew 16:19*
41   *Hebrews 10:25*

Planting implies depth. It suggests rootedness. It is imperative that you not only attend a local church but that you become truly rooted in a soul-winning local church.

There are many reasons to become rooted in the local church. **People find their purpose in church.** As a member of the church, you become a member of the body of Christ.[42] You become a part of continuing His work on the earth.

I Corinthians 12 explains how we are each a member. Just like the human body has many different parts; the eyes, the hands, the ears, etc., so the church has people who provide different functions, according to their design.

You play a key part in empowering the church when you find your place and begin to act according to your gifts. Just as a human body would be limited without a foot, the church is limited in its impact upon the world when Christians don't become planted in the church and play their part in reaching the lost, comforting the afflicted, and joining in corporate worship.

You now understand the importance of becoming planted in the local church. But how do you know if you've found a good church? What should you look for in joining a church? The following list is not exhaustive, but is a good profile for a great church:

---

42 *I Corinthians 12:12-28*

- A great church is a place where the whole family can go and grow. (Psalm 103:17)

- A great church challenges you to become a better person. A great church is not a feel better church, it's a be better church. (Hebrews 10:24)

- A great church has a vision to reach the lost. (Matthew 18:11)

- A great church is multi-generational. (Matthew 22:32)

Once you've found the local church that is right for you, and are beginning the process of being "planted", you must begin to find others and tell them the amazing things God has done in your life. You should invite them to church.

Remember that the church is made up of people, just like you. What does that mean? Well, for one thing, it means that it's not perfect. The church does have some people who are hypocrites…which means there's room for everyone! Jesus's love is so endless, He is not willing that any should perish – He wants everyone to know Him.

The reality is every Christian is working on becoming more like Christ but they will make mistakes. You will make mistakes. When mistakes are made, that's the most important moment to remain connected to the local church.

Because the church is God's plan for mankind, it's important to have reverence for it. He calls us "the body of Christ." We should love and respect the body of Christ.

In the physical sense, Joseph of Arimathea, a disciple of Jesus, showed us how to treat the body of Christ. After Jesus died on the cross, Joseph asked Pilate for Jesus's body.

He perfumed and wrapped Christ's body with delicate care. He preserved Christ's body.[43] When we "touch" the body of Christ by being planted in church, we should add to its purity and preservation. We should defend it and protect it because we love it. And we should add to it.

Jesus told his disciples, just before leaving earth, to tell others about Him. He told them to duplicate themselves[44] by teaching others everything He had taught them. He encouraged them to show kindness to all people, and to "love your neighbor as yourself."[45]

---

43   *John 19:38-42*
44   *Matthew 28:19-20*
45   *Mark 12:31*

Telling others about what Jesus did in your life is the greatest thing you can do. You were rescued and now you can help rescue others from a life of despair and emptiness.

Being a Christian means that you are just a beggar telling other beggars where you found the bread.[46]

We should be passionate about the local church. Once, Jesus defended the church and stopped evil that was happening in the church. There were men who were using the church for improper things and Jesus drove them out. In that moment, John 2:17 tells us, "His disciples remembered that it is written, '**Zeal for your house has consumed me**'."

Jesus was passionate about the church because it's God's plan – it's The Plan for bringing the body of Christ to life in the world.

Having a great church to bring others to is a part of the mission of God, and a fulfillment of your life's purpose. Get planted in a great local church and help others do the same. You'll discover health, strength and connection to God like you've never known before!

---

[46] *D.T. Niles*

Step Seven: Generosity

Being planted in the church means not only attending, but participating. You play your part by giving and serving. You build the church, and thus the impact of God in your community, by being generous with your time, talents, and money. When you are able to fulfill the call of God to share with the body of Christ, you will find yourself taking the final steps to becoming a mature, seasoned Christian.

Jesus taught his disciples to care for the less fortunate. To reach out to those who had little or no support. Jesus taught his disciples to give freely, for they had freely received all things from God[47].

What does it mean to "freely give"? **Freely** means "in a free manner; able to act at will." **Give** means, "to present voluntarily and without expecting compensation."[48] Freely giving means to give without thinking of what may come back to you. It also means giving without thinking of whether the recipient will make the best use of your gift. Once a gift is given, it's no longer yours. It's theirs.

---

47 *Matthew 10:8*
48 *American Heritage Dictionary*

Telling others about Jesus and freely showing compassion to your fellow man are the cornerstones of a Christian life. But God did not intend for these actions to happen in isolation.

God did not coin the phrase, as charming as it is, "practice random acts of kindness."

God is a God of order. He has a structure and a plan for advancing His work on the earth. If He left it up to the whims of man, it's highly unlikely that His will would be accomplished. So, when it comes to something as essential as financial support for the local church, God asks us to bring a specific percentage of our income to be used to pay for the daily functions of the church.

The specific type of giving God instituted is called tithing. Tithing is a word that simply means "a tenth." Another term for tithing is "first fruits." This comes from the very beginning of man, when Able the farmer, Adam and Eve's son, brought God the first and best of his crops as a way to show gratitude for God's blessing.

Jesus actually told the Pharisees, a group of religious zealots who eventually built the case for His death, that they did well by tithing.[49] God said to His people that they were to "bring the **whole tithe into the storehouse**."[50]

---

[49] *Matthew 23:23*
[50] *Malachi 3:10*

For a Christian, the storehouse is your local church. An important and powerful part of following Christ is tithing to your local church. **Bringing your tithe to God's House is as much a part of a Christian's life as prayer and reading the Bible.**

Tithing is actually not really giving. As the line above explains, tithing is *bringing*. You are simply bringing to God that which is already His.

Tithing was demonstrated even before the Law of God was given in the Old Testament.

Tithing continued after Jesus came and is an essential part of resourcing the work of the local church.

Beyond tithing, we begin to truly give when we make "offerings" to God. Offerings are financial contributions above and beyond the 10% tithe that we are commanded by God to bring.

Offerings can take many forms. They can be money for a missions project, for a building project. Offerings can be supporting a teenager for summer Bible camp. There are many different ways that offerings happen. An offering is simply giving that is separate from the tithe. **And an offering is our opportunity to truly show gratitude to God for His blessings, and to enable the church to engage in projects and missions beyond the basic functions of daily church management.**

Giving money is important and essential for the church to thrive, but giving money is not the only requirement for a Christian who seeks to fully engage in this walk of following Jesus every day.

Giving time and talents to the work of the church is just as important. In some cases, it's more important, because some people can give money more easily than time. Some people can write a check but never seem willing to use their talents to help the church improve and grow.

We demonstrate our heart toward God through our willingness to serve Him "with gladness."[51] Volunteering your abilities and your time serving in the local church is a powerful act of worship. It is also a clear demonstration to God of your love for Him and surrender to His will.

Psalm 84:10 says, "…I would rather be a doorkeeper in the church than live in the houses of the wicked." This verse illustrates how wonderful it is to serve God. Being a lowly servant in the house of God is better than living the high life in the homes of wicked people.

It's true. Serving God brings joy and fulfillment. It brings purpose. When you join a greeting team, the choir, the maintenance team, or any other essential service element of your local church, you get to be a part of setting the stage for those who don't yet know Jesus to find Him.

---

51   *Psalm 100:2*

When you give and serve in your local church, you soon discover and agree with the psalmist who wrote, "I was glad when they said to me, Let us go to the house of the Lord!"

Find a good local church. Get Planted.

Give. Don't just bring your tithe, but give an offering.

Serve. Give your time and talents to help your church be a powerful witness to the community and play your part in bringing new people to hear the gospel of Jesus Christ.

As the introduction to this book states, It doesn't matter where you're at on the path of life, it doesn't matter what you've done or where you're from. Jesus is your Savior, and that means the journey ahead is brighter. It won't be perfect. There will still be potholes, but you will never again walk alone.

Now you know not only where to walk but how to walk. Follow these steps and accelerate your pace. It's time to walk the Walk. It's time to follow Jesus Every Day. The steps outlined in this book are the key elements for living the Christian Walk, and succeeding at following Jesus every day.

Review these regularly and be reminded of how far you've come along life's path, and be inspired by how far you can go when you trust Jesus, gain power from the Holy Spirit, and continue The Walk.

Salvation: Romans 10:9

Water Baptism: Matthew 28:19

Baptism of the Holy Spirit: Acts 19:6

Bible Study: Joshua 1:8, Psalm 119:11

Daily Prayer: 1 Thessalonians 5:17

Local Church: Hebrews 10:25

Giving & Serving: Malachi 3:10, Psalm 100:2

About the Author

Steve Kelly is the Senior Pastor of Wave Church, a Christian church with national and international influence. Wave Church's two main campuses are in Virginia Beach, Virginia. It has multi-site campuses located throughout the state of Virginia, as well as North Carolina, with more to come.

Pastor Steve's passion is to win the lost and to lead the generations to find their purpose in Christ, through the building of the local church. Wave Church's primary mission is to help people do life well and find their purpose in Christ through being planted in the local church.

Made in the USA
Columbia, SC
05 February 2021